# Hello, Hedgehog

By Laura Buller

**Editors** Kathleen Teece, Abhijit Dutta
**Editorial Assistant** Seeta Parmar
**US Senior Editor** Shannon Beatty
**Senior Art Editor** Ann Cannings
**Project Art Editor** Roohi Rais
**Jacket Coordinator** Issy Walsh
**Jacket Designer** Ann Cannings
**DTP Designer** Dheeraj Singh
**Senior DTP Designer** Jagtar Singh
**Picture Researcher** Nimesh Agrawal
**Producer, Pre-Production** David Almond
**Senior Producer** Ena Matagic
**Managing Editors** Laura Gilbert, Monica Saigal
**Deputy Managing Art Editor** Ivy Sengupta
**Managing Art Editor** Diane Peyton Jones
**Delhi Team Head** Malavika Talukder
**Creative Director** Helen Senior
**Publishing Director** Sarah Larter

**Reading Consultant** Linda Gambrell Ph.D.
**Subject Consultant** Jill Nelson

First American Edition, 2019
Published in the United States by DK Publishing
1450 Broadway, Suite 801, New York, NY 10018


19 20 21 22 23 10 9 8 7 6 5 4 3 2 1
001–316570–Dec/2019


Published in Great Britain by Dorling Kindersley Limited

A catalog record for this book
is available from the Library of Congress.
ISBN: 978-1-4654-9059-9 (Paperback)
ISBN: 978-1-4654-9060-5 (Hardcover)



Printed and bound in China

The publisher would like to thank the following for their kind permission to reproduce their photographs:
(Key: a-above; b-below/bottom; c-center; f-far; l-left; r-right; t-top)

**1 Alamy Stock Photo:** Incamerastock (b). **3 123RF.com:** Pstedrak (b). **4–5 Dreamstime.com:** Tchara (b). **6–7 Alamy Stock Photo:** Avalon / Photoshot License (t). **8–9 123RF.com:** Alekss (b). **10 Alamy Stock Photo:** Arco Images GmbH. **11 Dreamstime.com:** Ondřej Prosický (cb). **13 Dreamstime.com:** Gualtiero Boffi (clb); Vasiliy Vishnevskiy (tl). **iStockphoto.com:** Neil Bowman (cra). **14–15 Dreamstime.com:** Isselee (bc); Laboko. **14 Dreamstime.com:** Isselee (bc/Baby Hedgehog, bc). **16–17 naturepl.com:** Klein & Hubert (t). **18–19 Alamy Stock Photo:** Juniors Bildarchiv GmbH (b). **20–21 iStockphoto.com:** Sandorgora (t). **22 Alamy Stock Photo:** Blickwinkel (b). **23 Alamy Stock Photo:** Imagebroker (t). **24–25 Getty Images:** Dieter Hopf (b). **26 Getty Images:** Ingo Arndt / Nature Picture Library (t). **27 Dreamstime.com:** Sergii Myronenko (cb). **28 Dreamstime.com:** Bartek Trojniak (cb). **29 Depositphotos Inc:** Chris2766 (cb). **Dreamstime.com:** Martina889 (t). **31 123RF.com:** James Cumming. **32 123RF.com:** Guido Sobbe (t). **33 Alamy Stock Photo:** Mark Williams (t). **34 Dreamstime.com:** Ondřej Prosický (b). **35 Alamy Stock Photo:** Víctor Suárez (t). **37 Dreamstime.com:** Anney P. **38 Dreamstime.com:** Genta27 (cb). **39 Alamy Stock Photo:** Sam Stephenson (t). **40–41 Alamy Stock Photo:** The Photolibrary Wales (b). **41 Dreamstime.com:** Mingis (t). **42 Alamy Stock Photo:** Universal Images Group North America LLC / DeAgostini (cr). **Dreamstime.com:** Farinoza (bl). **43 Avalon:** NHPA (crb). **Dreamstime.com:** Kamonrutm (clb).

**Endpaper images:** *Front:* **Dreamstime.com:** Anney P; *Back:* **Dreamstime.com:** Anney P

**Cover images:** *Front:* **Alamy Stock Photo:** Coatsey c; **Dorling Kindersley:** *Neil Fletcher t*

# Contents

4 Chapter 1: Meet the hedgehog

12 *Around the world*

14 Chapter 2: Growing up

22 Chapter 3: Nighttime adventure

28 *Hibernation*

30 Chapter 4: Prickly protection

36 Chapter 5: Hedgehog preservation

42 *Family tree*

44 Quiz

46 Glossary

47 Index

# Chapter 1
# Meet the hedgehog

Look! There's something brown and fuzzy over there in the grass. Is it a pine cone?

Peek a little bit closer. The round, bumpy ball is moving.

Prickly spikes point in every direction. A long nose pokes out and wiggles as it sniffs the air. A small, cone-shaped face appears. Little arms and feet stretch out. Slowly, the ball starts to uncurl. It's a hedgehog!

Hedgehogs live in many places, from woodlands and deserts to backyards. Some build a nest from leaves and twigs.

Others hide away in holes in the ground. Some hedgehogs can curl up to be the size of a tennis ball.

Wherever they live, most hedgehogs look alike. Almost every part of a hedgehog's body is covered in pointy spines.

Even though hedgehogs have big, dark eyes, they can't see very well.

Hedgehog spines are hollow.

They figure out what's going on around them by listening with their excellent ears, and smelling with their twitchy noses.

A long snout
helps the hedgehog
to find food.

A hedgehog's nose is so twitchy because smelling helps it to survive. Inside a hedgehog's nose, a special part helps it to "taste" smells in the air. It sniffs out food when it goes hunting at night.

Hedgehogs eat all sorts of things, including mushrooms!

# Around the world

There are 17 different species of hedgehog around the world.

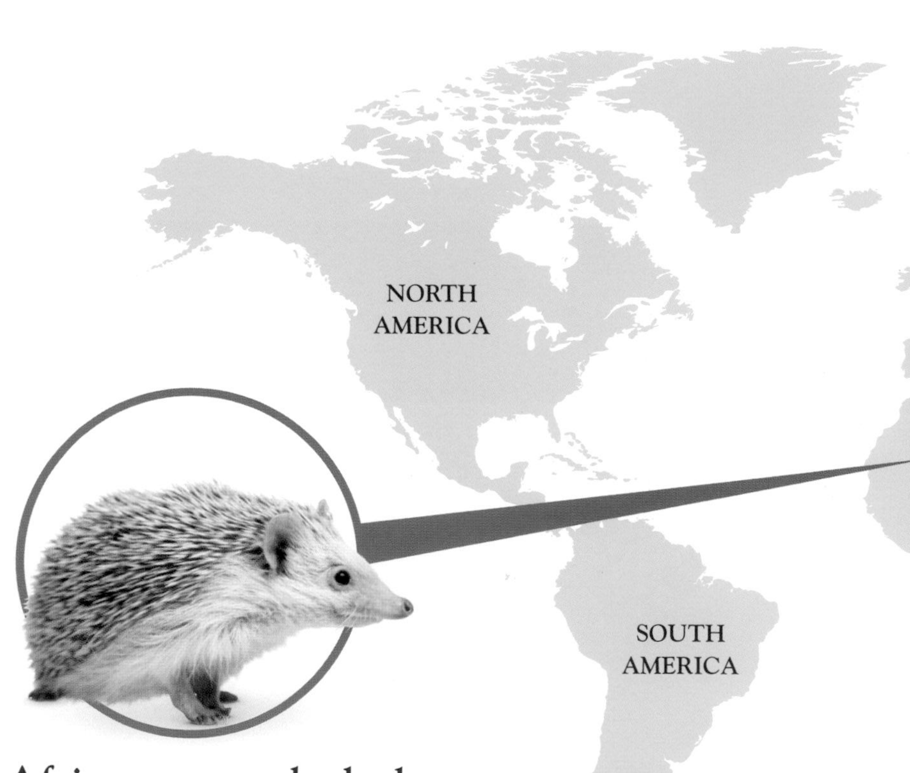


**African pygmy hedgehog**
This little creature lives in the savannas of Africa.

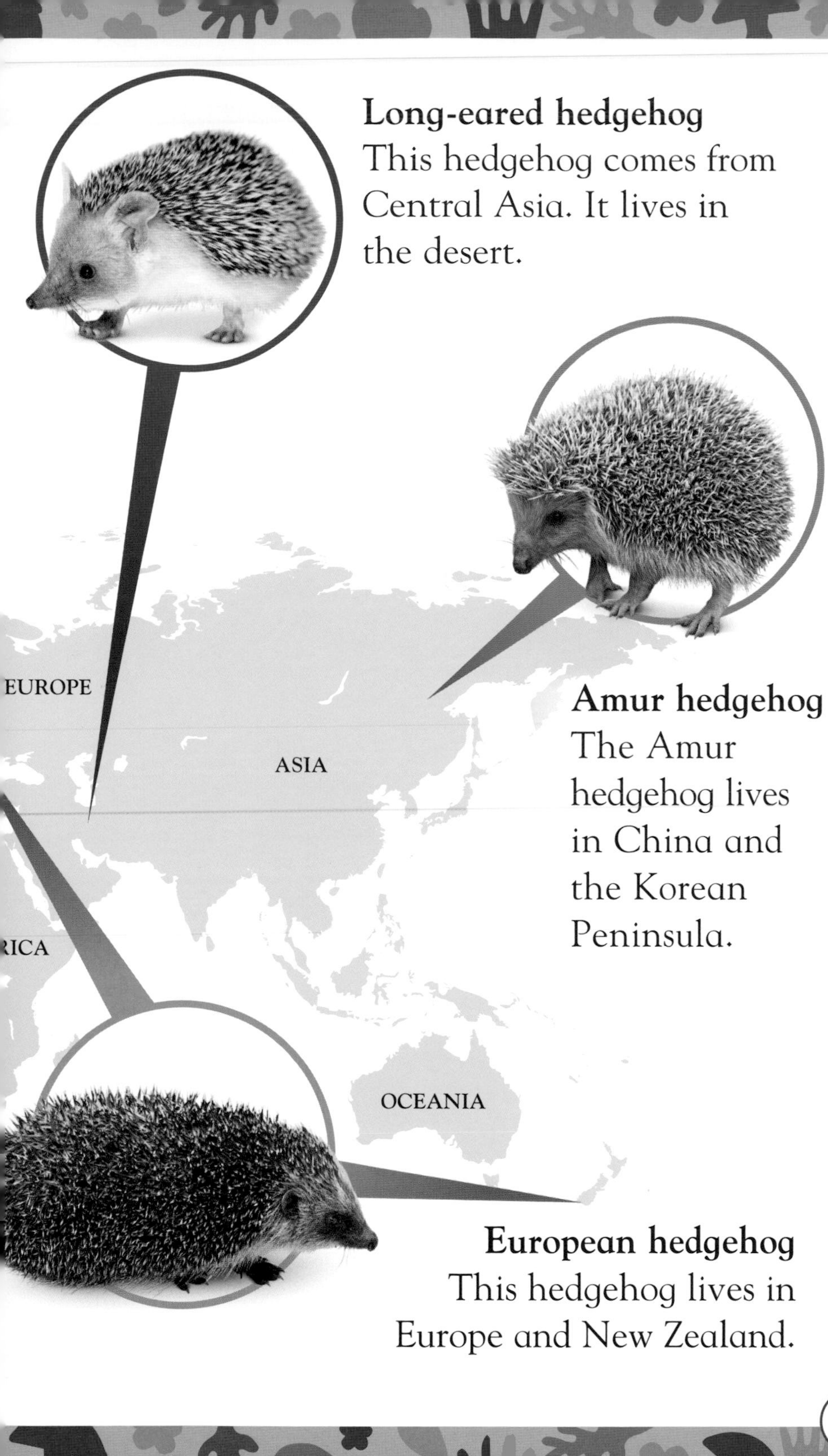


**Long-eared hedgehog**
This hedgehog comes from Central Asia. It lives in the desert.

**Amur hedgehog**
The Amur hedgehog lives in China and the Korean Peninsula.

**European hedgehog**
This hedgehog lives in Europe and New Zealand.

# Chapter 2
# Growing up

A mother hedgehog gives birth to babies, called hoglets. There may be four or five tiny hoglets in each litter.

A few soft, white spines cover their pink, wrinkly bodies. The newborns cannot see or curl into balls yet. Their mother looks after them and keeps them safe. A hoglet's eyes open after two weeks.

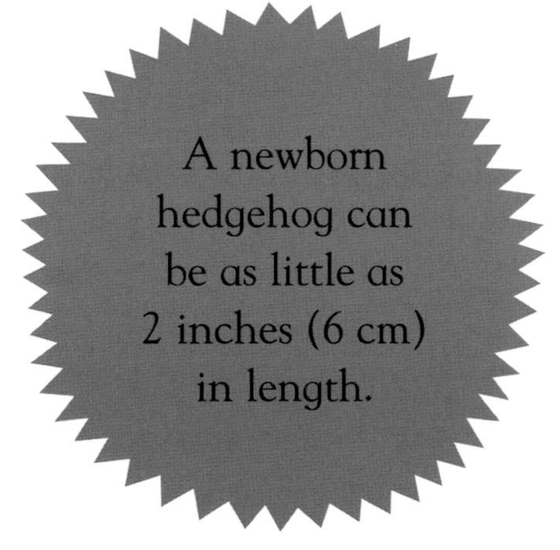

The hoglets stay inside their nests of leaves and grass for now. They drink their mother's milk. In just a few days, the first pointy brown spines begin to show.

Hoglets grow about 150 spines within a day of birth.

The hoglets grow stronger and bigger. Fuzzy fur covers their small bodies. Soon, they open their eyes for the first time. Hello, world!

Their mother takes the hoglets outside for a look around when they are about a month old. The young hoglets no longer drink their mother's milk. She shows them how to hunt for food.

Now they are strong enough to roll into a ball if they sense danger.

A hoglet makes whistling sounds when it is scared.

Hoglets grow up quickly once they're shown how to hunt. They head out to live alone at the age of around five or six weeks.

Females are ready to have babies of their own when they are about two years old. Males start to follow them around in big circles, loudly sniffing and snorting.

# Chapter 3 Nighttime adventure

Shhh! Something is asleep, even though the sun is shining. A hedgehog usually stays in its nest all day long. It curls up into a spiny ball.

Hedgehogs can sleep for up to 18 hours a day!

When the sun goes down, the hedgehog uncurls itself. It gets ready to leave the nest and look for food.

Sniff, sniff! The hedgehog trundles along with its nose close to the ground. It is sniffing for food. Most hedgehogs like to eat worms, bugs, and snails.

When they find an insect hiding in the grass, hedgehogs use their noses to poke right in. They grab their prey with pointy teeth.

Hedgehogs have up to 44 teeth.

Never give hedgehogs milk because it makes them very sick.

They don't just eat one meal, though. Hedgehogs keep hunting long into the night. In one evening, they can travel as far as 1.2 miles (2 km).

These prickly pals usually stay low to the ground as they move. They climb over rocks and tree stumps in their way. Hedgehogs can also swim across rivers and ponds.

# Hibernation

During cold winters, hedgehogs may hibernate. This means going into a deep sleep that lasts until spring.

Before winter, hedgehogs eat a lot of food to make themselves fat.

As they snooze, the stored fat gives them energy. It also keeps them warm.

When the weather gets warmer, they wake up. They start looking for food again.

# Chapter 4 Prickly protection

A hedgehog shuffles along. It is time to head back to its nest for some sleep. Yet, just at the edge of the woods, a hungry fox waits.

The fox gets ready to leap at the hedgehog. Just in time, the hedgehog smells its enemy… and danger! How will it escape?

Foxes can be
dangerous to hoglets,
who cannot protect
themselves.

Adult hedgehogs can have around 5,000–7,000 spines.

The hedgehog has a secret weapon. Thousands of spines cover its back. They are made of the same material as our hair and fingernails.

When it gets scared, a hedgehog points its spines out in every direction. Then, it uses its muscles to curl up into a spiky ball. This protects its soft belly.

The fox sniffs around but doesn't want to get pricked. It trots back into the woods to find a less spiky treat.

When at risk, a hedgehog can run as fast as a human walking quickly.

Phew! The hedgehog unrolls itself. To get back to its nest in a hurry, it stretches its legs and makes a run for it.

# Chapter 5
# Hedgehog preservation

Hedgehogs live in the countryside, and in towns and cities. Most people like having hedgehogs in their backyards. This is because hedgehogs gobble up slugs and other small animals that like to eat plants.

However, some people put chemicals in their backyard to kill slugs. This can end up harming the hedgehogs who eat the slugs.

Hedgehogs are often called the gardener's friend.

Even if humans are very careful with them, hedgehogs may still be afraid. They have sharp teeth, and may nip at you.

Hedgehogs have four types of teeth, just like human beings.

A hedgehog is nursed back to health at Brent Lodge Animal Hospital, West Sussex, UK.

Some might carry germs that can harm you or your pets. If you are lucky enough to see a hedgehog, it's best to look, but not touch.

The UK has lost a third of its hedgehogs in the last 20 years. People are destroying hedgehogs' woodland homes to build their own houses and farms. Crossing roads can be risky for these little creatures.

A man making a nest for hedgehogs in his yard.

Conservation groups (people who want to protect hedgehogs) do lots to help. They teach people how to make their backyards into hedgehog-friendly zones.

# Family tree

Hedgehogs are part of a family of animals called Erinaceidae (Eh-ri-NAY-sha-die).

**Porcupine**
Porcupines and hedgehogs are not related. They live, eat, and behave differently.

**Deinogalerix (Die-no-ga-le-rix)**

This creature was twice as long as the hedgehog. It lived between 10 and 7 million years ago.

Erinaceidae

Hedgehog

Hedgehogs first appeared 15 million years ago. People used to think hedgehogs carried fruit on their spines!

Moonrat

This mammal is covered in thick fur instead of spines. It lives on tropical islands.

# Quiz

1. What species of hedgehog is found in the wild in New Zealand?

2. How many different hedgehog species are there?

3. What are baby hedgehogs called?

4. How old are baby hedgehogs when they leave the nest?

5. What do hedgehogs like to eat?

6. Are hedgehogs more active during the day or at night?

7 True or false: hedgehogs are good swimmers.

8 How many spines does an adult hedgehog have?

9 How far can a hedgehog travel in one night?

10 At what age can hedgehogs have babies?

**Answers to the quiz:**

**1.** The European hedgehog; **2.** 17; **3.** Hoglets; **4.** About a month old; **5.** Hedgehogs eat worms, bugs, and snails; **6.** At night; **7.** True!; **8.** 5,000–7,000; **9.** Up to 1.2 miles (2 km); **10.** Two years old

# Glossary

**conservation**
The protection of everything in nature.

**desert**
A habitat that gets very little rain throughout the year.

**habitat**
The home of an animal or plant.

**mammal**
A warm-blooded animal that makes milk to feed its young.

**mating**
When a male and female animal come together and make babies.

**savanna**
A flat, grassy, and dry habitat with few trees.

**species**
The different types of animal in the same family.

# Index

African pygmy hedgehog 12
Amur hedgehog 13
birth 15, 21
conservation 40–41
defenses 32–33
desert 6, 13
diet 11, 18, 25, 26, 29, 36
Erinaceidae 42–43
European hedgehog 13
fox 30–31, 33, 34
hibernation 28–29
hoglets 14–15, 16–17, 18–19, 20–21, 31
long-eared hedgehog 13
mating 20–21
moonrat 43
nest 16, 22, 35
porcupine 42
savanna 12
spines 8, 15, 32–33
swimming 27
teeth 25, 38
woodland 6

# A LEVEL FOR EVERY READER

This book is a part of an exciting four-level reading series to support children in developing the habit of reading widely for both pleasure and information. Each book is designed to develop a child's reading skills, fluency, grammar awareness, and comprehension in order to build confidence and enjoyment when reading.

**Ready for a Level 2 (Beginning to Read) book**

A child should:

- be able to recognize a bank of common words quickly and be able to blend sounds together to make some words.
- be familiar with using beginner letter sounds and context clues to figure out unfamiliar words.
- sometimes correct his/her reading if it doesn't look right or make sense.
- be aware of the need for a slight pause at commas and a longer one at periods.

**A valuable and shared reading experience**

For many children, reading requires much effort, but adult participation can make reading both fun and easier. Here are a few tips on how to use this book with a young reader:

*Check out the contents together:*

- read about the book on the back cover and talk about the contents page to help heighten interest and expectation.
- discuss new or difficult words.
- chat about labels, annotations, and pictures.

*Support the reader:*

- give the book to the young reader to turn the pages.
- where necessary, encourage longer words to be broken into syllables, sound out each one, and then flow the syllables together; ask him/her to reread the sentence to check the meaning.
- encourage the reader to vary his/her voice as he/she reads; demonstrate how to do this if helpful.

*Talk at the end of each book, or after every few pages:*

- ask questions about the text and the meaning of the words used—this helps develop comprehension skills.
- read the quiz at the end of the book and encourage the reader to answer the questions, if necessary, by turning back to the relevant pages to find the answers.

Series consultant, Dr. Linda Gambrell, Distinguished Professor of Education at Clemson University, has served as President of the National Reading Conference, the College Reading Association, and the International Reading Association.